SHOW-ME-HOW
I Can Make Things
How-to-make craft projects
for the very young

SALLY WALTON

INDEX

For Rupert and Roxy, and with thanks to Leonie

First published in 1995 by Lorenz Books

Lorenz Books is an imprint of
Anness Publishing Limited
1 Boundary Row
London SE1 8HP

First published in Australia in 1995
by Koala Book Company
722 Bourke St, Redfern
N.S.W. 2016, Australia

ISBN 1 85967 064 4

A CIP catalogue record for this book
is available from the British Library.

Editorial Director: Joanna Lorenz
Project Editor: Clare Nicholson
Designer: Peter Butler
Photographer: John Freeman

Printed and bound in China

PLEASE NOTE
**The level of adult supervision needed will
depend on the abilities and age of the
children following the projects. However,
we advise that adult supervision is always
preferable, and vital if the project calls
for the use of sharp knives or other utensils.
Always keep potentially dangerous tools
and products well out of the reach of
young children.**

ACKNOWLEDGEMENTS
The publishers would like to thank the following
children for appearing in this book, and of course
their parents: Kirsty Fraser, Reece Harle,
Edward and Thomas Hogarth, Saadia Jacobs,
Jade Jeffries, Ephram Lovemore, Tania Murphy,
Rupert and Roxy Walton, and George Wheeler.
Also Binney and Smith for lending Crayola products.

Contents

Introduction

Making things is great fun and very rewarding. It takes time and you have to concentrate to understand how things are put together. But all the hard work is worth it, because when you have made a rattlesnake or painted a flowerpot, it has some of your own very special magic in it. You will feel so proud, and everyone will admire your work. Once you understand how to make a mobile or cut flowers from felt, you will always know how it is done. Then you will be able to make up new designs of your own.

Look at the photographs of the children making up each project. They show you each stage and the words explain what they are doing. You can do it too, just follow what the children do.

Remember to ask a grown-up for permission before you begin making things. There are some projects that need a grown-up's help. Leave all the dangerous cutting-out to a grown-up, and never use a craft knife on your own as they are very dangerous. You may have to remind grown-ups that you are the one making things, because once they get started on the projects, they may not want to stop!

Be a crafty collector

We all like to recycle as much as possible. Once you start making things, you will be watching out to see what can be saved from the dustbin and made into a toy or a gift. You will need a good strong box for your collection and somewhere to store it. If you save milk cartons and yogurt pots, give them a good wash in soapy water and dry them well, otherwise they may get smelly. Old tins and bottles are often covered with labels which you will want to take off. The easiest way to do this is to fill a washing-up bowl with some warm water and soak the bottle in the water for approximately ten minutes. The label should peel off very easily. Collect small cardboard boxes and tubes, lollipop sticks, safe-edged tins, straws, corks, string, shells, bottle tops and cotton reels.

It is important to know when to stop collecting. If you have enough recycled packaging to fill your box, then start making things!

Colourful materials

For some projects you may have to use materials which you don't have at home, such as coloured card, felt, tissue paper, beads, pipe cleaners and wrapping paper. If you buy something special for a project then always keep any left-over scraps as they are bound to come in handy for any other project in the future.

Keeping clean

When you make things you can also make a lot of mess! It is most important to start off by protecting your work surface with old newspapers. Or putting down a tablecloth that will wipe clean. Do this first, because once you get involved with a project, it is easy not to notice the mess that you are making.

Wear an overall, apron or a big, old shirt to protect your clothes when you are painting. Before you start, roll up your sleeves as high as possible as they have a habit of dangling in paint pots and glue!

Getting started

When you have decided which projects you are going to make, collect together all the materials and equipment you will need and lay them out on your work surface. You will then find it much easier to work.

Clearing up

When you have finished, always clear up and put away all your things. Ask a grown-up to help you if you need to, but don't just leave a mess behind. Keep your equipment in good order and you will be ready to make something else another day.

Equipment

All the projects in this book can be made easily at home. There are some basic pieces of equipment which you will need for nearly all of the projects, such as scissors, glue and paints or felt-tipped pens. If you look after your basic equipment well it will last for a long time and you will be able to make lots and lots of the projects.

PVA glue

This glue has many other names. You may know it as white glue, school glue, or woodworking glue. It is water-based, which means that your hands and brushes come clean under the tap. It is white, so that you can see where you have put it, but it becomes clear when it dries, so any mistakes are invisible. PVA glue sticks most things together – wood, cardboard, paper, cloth and plastic. It is great for applying glitter too – just mix it in and paint it on. You can apply the glue with either a paintbrush or a glue spreader.

You can make a varnish by mixing PVA glue with water. Use three parts of PVA glue to one part water. Paint this onto clay flowerpots to make a waterproof surface to paint on. Papier-mâché used to be made with wallpaper paste, but this contains chemicals that can be harmful to your skin. A PVA glue and water mixture used with newspaper makes very strong papier-mâché and the glue can be used undiluted on parts that need extra strength, like the handle for the maracas.

Paints

There are lots of different kinds of paint, and it is important to use the sort that is best for the job you are doing. Sometimes pale watery colours are perfect and other times you need strong bright colours that will cover up printing or pictures on a recycled package.

The paint recommended for making things is acrylic. It can be mixed with water, to make it runny, or used straight from the tube or pot to give a solid, bold colour. You can wash your brush out under the tap, but you must remember to do it straight away, because acrylic paint dries very quickly, and brushes will spoil if they are not cleaned before the paint dries. Stand your brushes in a jar of water until you wash them out.

Household paint called emulsion is good to use as an undercoat. On the canal boat and the doll's house, emulsion paint was used first to block out all the writing and pictures, then the acrylic paint on top made a bright solid colour coating. You can buy acrylic paints from stationery shops

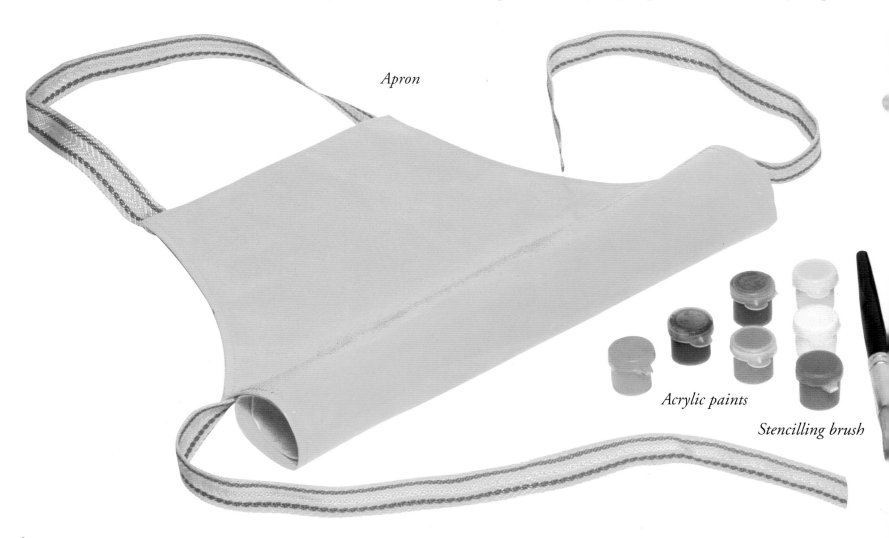

Apron

Acrylic paints

Stencilling brush

and art and craft shops where they also sell acrylic gloss varnish, used in some of the projects. In addition, you will need special fabric paints to decorate the felt on the jewellery box and the mussels for the mobile.

It is sometimes difficult to buy paints in a wide range of colours so why not try mixing your own – red and blue will make purple, red and yellow will make orange, and red, green and yellow will make brown. You can also make all sorts of different shades of reds, blues, greens, yellows and greys by mixing white in with the paints you have bought.

Paint pots
These are special paint pots with lids to stop you spilling the paint! They are very useful if you need to mix up a large amount of paint or to dilute paint with water. They come with lots of different coloured lids so you can match the colour of the paint to the lid. Always wash out the pots thoroughly before putting a different colour in them. If you are using undiluted paints in small amounts you can put them in a paint palette.

Paintbrushes
Paintbrushes come in many different shapes and sizes. Use thin, pointed brushes for painting fine lines and thick or flat-ended brushes for large areas. For stencilling you will need a short, fat brush with stiff hairs.

Take great care of your paintbrushes, and try not to damage them by being rough. If you move them in one direction this will keep them smooth and make them last longer. Always wash your brushes thoroughly after you have used them.

Apron
To prevent your clothes from getting covered in paint, wear a smock or an apron, or ask an adult for an old shirt. That way you can make as much mess as you like.

Ruler
This is useful for measuring and drawing straight lines.

Scissors
Scissors should not be too sharp and must be handled with safety in mind at all times. If you have to cut some thick cardboard and need sharper scissors, ask a grown-up to do the cutting for you.

Felt-tipped pens
Felt-tipped pens are always good to use on paper. The colours can't be mixed like paint, so it's best to use them separately.

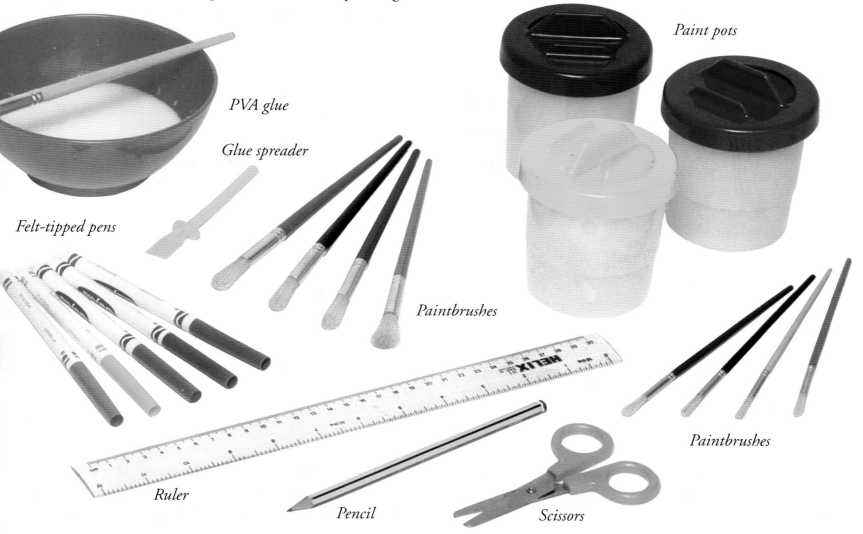

PVA glue

Glue spreader

Felt-tipped pens

Paint pots

Paintbrushes

Paintbrushes

Ruler

Pencil

Scissors

Templates

Some of the projects in this book have pattern templates for you to trace. You will find these on the opposite page.

1 Place a sheet of tracing paper over the template pattern in the book. Hold the paper in position with your spare hand. Carefully trace the pattern using a soft pencil.

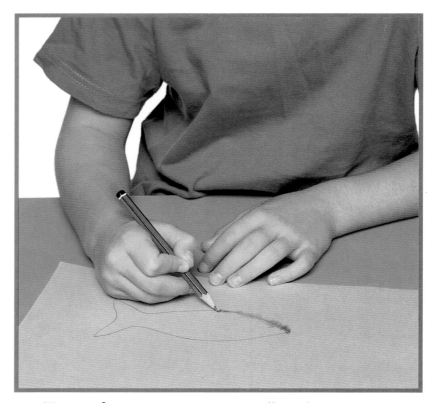

2 To transfer your pattern onto cardboard or paper, turn the tracing paper over and scribble over the outline with your pencil.

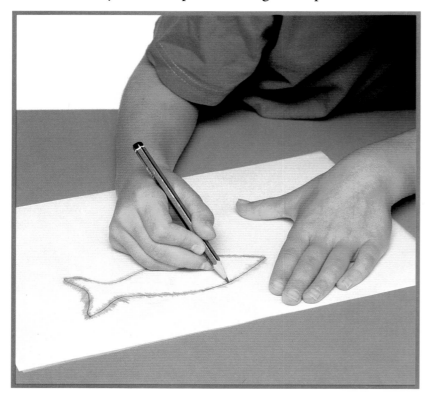

3 Turn the tracing paper over again and place it on your sheet of paper or cardboard. Draw around the outline of the pattern firmly. It will transfer onto the paper or cardboard.

4 Remove the tracing paper and make sure all the pattern has been transferred. Use scissors to cut out the template, and then draw around it as shown in the project pictures.

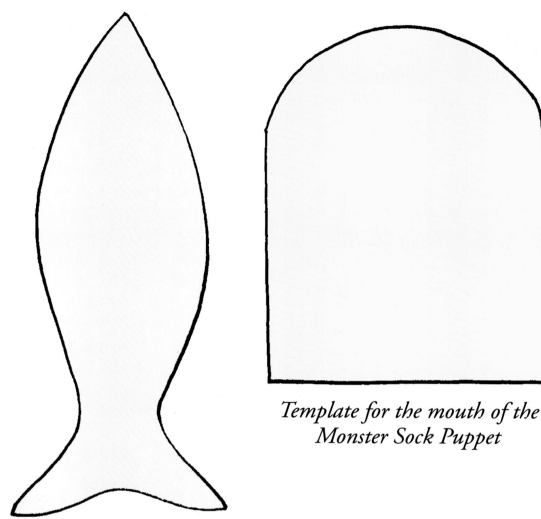

*Template for
Magnetic Fishing*

*Template for the mouth of the
Monster Sock Puppet*

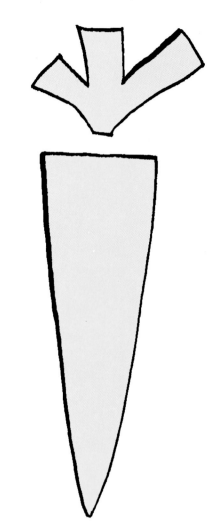

*Template for the
Stencilled Cork Place-mat*

Stencils and circles

When you are making the stencil for the table-mat, trace the template of the carrot from the book. Turn the tracing paper over and scribble over the outline with a pencil, as shown in step 2 on the opposite page. Turn the tracing paper over again and place it on a piece of cardboard, but make sure that it is in the middle of the cardboard. Draw around the outline firmly, see step 3. Remove the tracing paper and go over the outline to make sure the pattern is complete. To cut out the stencil, make a hole in the middle of the design then cut towards the outside edge. Move the scissors as you cut the design. You want to end up with a piece of cardboard with the pattern cut out of the middle. If you find it difficult to cut the stencil then ask an adult to cut it using a craft knife or some big scissors.

To draw circles, find a saucer, cup or any other round object which is about the right size. Place the object on your paper or cardboard and draw around it for a perfect circle.

Papier-mâché Maracas

First you make your maracas, and then you make your music. Playing the maracas is halfway between dancing and playing an instrument. You shake them, repeating the movement and the rest in-between, to make a rhythm - and it is not something you can do by standing still!

Maracas are played as part of the percussion section of a band. The ones they use are made from dried gourds that grow in hot countries. They are like small melons or squash and when hollowed out they dry as hard as wood. Once dry, they are partly filled with beans or beads.

Home-made music

Roxy and Rupert are making these maracas from papier-mâché. Newspaper is soaked in water and then pasted with a PVA glue and water mixture. First you cover a balloon with one layer of newsprint strips, then build up another layer and another until the paper is four or five layers thick. If you have trouble remembering which layer is which, use coloured tissue paper in-between the newsprint, then you will know where you are.

Leave the papier-mâché for a few days – it needs to be bone dry before you take the balloon out, otherwise it will collapse in a soggy mess! Be patient and you will soon have made your own musical instrument.

YOU WILL NEED THESE MATERIALS AND TOOLS

Old newspapers, torn into strips

Bowl of water

Balloon

20 cm (8 in) bamboo cane, for the handle

Paper funnel

Dried beans or beads, to put inside

Tissue paper, in a few colours

Gold stars

Also a cup, PVA glue, paintbrush and acrylic gloss (optional)

1 Soak strips of newspaper in a bowl of water overnight. You need at least five sheets, torn into strips about 2 – 3 cm (1 – 1¼ in) wide.

2 Blow up a balloon to about the size of a large orange. Stand it in a cup and begin to cover it with a layer of soaked, pasted paper strips. Mix PVA and water in equal amounts for the paste.

3 Take some long strips of newspaper and paste them with undiluted PVA glue. Wind them around the bamboo. Leave 6 cm (2½ in) uncovered, and make a ball shape where the covering stops. When dry cover with more strips.

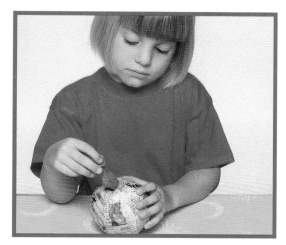

4 Pull up the end of the balloon and burst it, then pull the balloon out of the papier-mâché.

5 Place the paper funnel in the hole, then carefully pour in some beans or beads.

6 Fix in the handle by gluing all around the hole and the round part of the handle then push the two together. Make one more strip of newspaper, cover it with PVA paste, and wind it around the join as a collar. Cover with soaked and pasted strips till smooth. Leave to dry.

7 Cover with a layer of torn blue tissue paper and then add diamond shapes in different colours that have been dipped in the PVA and water mixture.

8 Stick on the gold stars and give a final varnish with acrylic gloss or PVA glue and water mixed three parts glue to one part water.

Make music with maracas.

Canal Boat

Canals are like roads made out of water. They were used to move all kinds of factory goods from one part of the country to another on long, low canal boats, called barges. A long time ago the canals were very busy, but now most factories use lorries or trains instead. People still use the canals and barges, but mostly as homes or for holidays. The barge people have always decorated their boats in the same way, using black, red, yellow and green paint. They would paint flowers and patterns on the barge itself and all their buckets, flower-pots, jugs and boxes. The skill of barge painting was passed down through families, and people took great pride in their painted boats.

YOU WILL NEED THESE
MATERIALS AND TOOLS

Tall milk or juice carton, with a pointed end

Pegs

Cork

Bottle cap

Also scissors, ruler, pencil, black emulsion paint, white emulsion paint (optional), red acrylic paint, paintbrushes, PVA glue, strips of white paper 1 – 1.5 cm (about ½ in) wide, felt-tipped pens and acrylic varnish (optional)

Beautiful barges

Edward has decorated this barge in the traditional colours, but using felt-tipped pens to make the patterns. Every barge has a name, usually a pretty girl's name, like Jenny-Wren or Lindy-Lou. Choose a name for your canal boat.

1 Cut the carton in half lengthways. One half will be the boat. Cut off the ends of the other half, to leave a rectangle of card. This will be the roof of the barge.

2 To make the roof, measure 1.5 cm (about ½ in) either side of both the existing creases and score lines with a blunt pencil and ruler. The lines will make it easier to fold the card.

3 Paint the outside of the boat black and the inside too if you wish. The top can be painted white first. This will make the red much brighter. If not, just give the top two coats of red acrylic paint.

4 Fold the roof along the lines and glue the edges to the inner sides of the boat. Peg until the glue is dry.

5 Ask a grown-up to cut a cork in half lengthways. Paint the two halves black. When they are dry, glue one half across the back of the boat and one onto the back of the roof. Glue the bottle cap onto the front of the roof, as a funnel.

6 Decorate the paper strips with felt-tipped pens. Use red, yellow and green to make patterns, and write the name of your barge on the long strips if you wish. Draw windows and some flowers for the top, as bright and bold as you like.

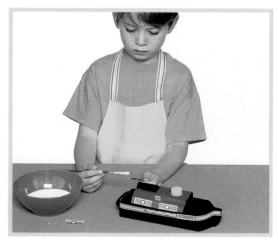

7 Stick all the paper strip decorations to the boat with PVA glue. If you want to put the boat in water, give it a coat of acrylic varnish for protection.

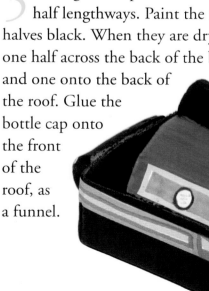

A real work of recycled art.

Giant Sunflower Card

Sunflowers are among the tallest plants that we grow in our gardens, and this card takes its unusual shape from them. A sunflower has bright yellow petals and a big, rounded brown centre packed with seeds. This is the special part of the card that Kirsty is making.

This card would make a lovely present for Mother's Day, or a special gift for your teacher. Envelopes this shape may be diffi-cult to find, so wrap up your card as a present. That is, if you can bear to part with it!

YOU WILL NEED THESE MATERIALS AND TOOLS

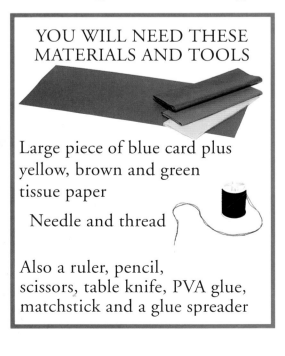

Large piece of blue card plus yellow, brown and green tissue paper

Needle and thread

Also a ruler, pencil, scissors, table knife, PVA glue, matchstick and a glue spreader

Tricky and sticky

The seed centre is the trickiest part of the sunflower to make, but once you understand how it is done, you will be making them all the time. The most important thing to remember is that too much glue will spread through the fine tissue paper and stick the next layer as well, and then the pop-up won't work. So use a tiny dot of glue, carefully pinching the two pieces of tissue paper between your finger and thumb to stick them together.

If you want to have leaves with jagged edges ask an adult to cut them out with pinking shears.

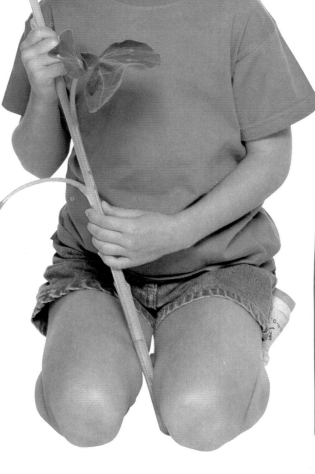

1 Cut out the card to 22 x 56 cm (8½ x 22 in). Find the middle, and score the card using a blunt table knife against a ruler. Just press firmly, so that the knife dents the card.

2 Fold the brown tissue paper over so that you have 10 layers. Cut out a circle that measures about 10 cm (4 in) across. Use a needle and thread to sew a running stitch down the centre line.

3 Cut out the petals, leaves and stems. You will need a lot of petals, about 30 to start with, two stems and five leaves.

4 To make the centre, think of a clockface. Imagine that the stitches go from 9 to 3. Using the matchstick, put a dot of glue at 12 o'clock.

5 Fold over the first layer of tissue and pinch it together where the dot of glue is.

6 Then, make two dots on the next layer of tissue. These go at where the 10 and 2 would be on the clock. Pinch together to stick. The next dot goes on the 12 spot and after that the 10 and the 2 again. Keep going like this until you reach the last layer. Let it dry.

7 Draw a circle for the flower centre, and arrange the petals around it. Put a thin layer of glue on each one. Make two or three circles of petals.

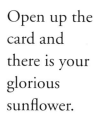

8 Spread a stripe of glue down the centre line and stick the two stems on top of each other. Stick down the leaves and the flower centre in the circle.

Open up the card and there is your glorious sunflower.

Stencilled Cork Place-mat

Make this place-mat, and brighten up the dinner table, even before the food arrives. It looks so good that the whole family will want one, and you will have to make a matching set. Start by making one for yourself. Ephram has used a carrot design for his mat. He could make a set using different vegetable stencils for each mat.

Stencilling technique

Stencilling is great fun and easy to do if you remember two simple rules. Always hold the stencil firmly in place with your spare hand and never use too much paint on your brush. The paint needs to be thick, so don't mix any water with it. Dip your brush in and then dab it on a piece of kitchen paper before you stencil on the cork tile. Use a different brush for each colour.

The felt backing will protect the table surface and also strengthen the thin cork and stop it breaking if you bend it. If you like a glossy surface, finish off your mat with a coat of acrylic gloss varnish, or PVA glue and water mixed three parts to one. This will add a tough, wipe-clean surface to the mat.

YOU WILL NEED THESE MATERIALS AND TOOLS

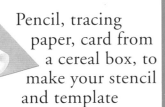

Unsealed cork floor tile and orange felt

Pencil, tracing paper, card from a cereal box, to make your stencil and template

Also a ruler, craft knife, scissors, black marker pen (not water-colour), thick, soft stencil brush, acrylic paint – orange and green, kitchen paper towel, acrylic var-nish, PVA glue and a paintbrush

1 Using a pencil and ruler, measure and draw a line about 10 cm (4 in) in from the cork tile edge. Ask a grown-up to cut this strip off for you with a craft knife.

2 Find the carrot stencil pattern in the introduction, trace it onto the card and cut it out. Use the scissors to make a hole in the middle of the design, and then cut towards the outside edge. Move the card towards the scissors as you cut.

3 Make a template of the zig-zag border from the card. It should be the same length as the long side of the mat. Use the black marker pen to draw around it and colour the shape in. Fill in the corners to make triangles.

4 Stencil the carrots, starting with the one in the middle. Work from the stencil card inwards towards the centre, using a light dabbing movement. Always dab the paint from the pot onto a kitchen paper towel before using the brush on the cork. Use the paint very sparingly. You can always go over it again to add more colour, but too much at first will make blobs. Wipe the back of your stencil before painting the next carrot. The paint will dry quickly, but wait until it has done so or you may smudge the pattern.

5 To protect the design, either coat it with a glossy acrylic varnish or a coat of PVA glue mixed with water, three parts to one.

7 Spread the felt with PVA. Make sure that you reach right up to the edges. Stick this to the back of the cork.

6 Cut the orange felt so that it is the same size as the mat.

More Stencilling Ideas

If you are more likely to eat your dinner from a tray, then you could paint it in the same way. If you have an old tray at home, ask whether you may decorate it. A wooden tray will need rubbing down with sandpaper first, and a tin tray may need a coat of gloss paint before you stencil it. You could use fabric paints to stencil onto plain dinner napkins, or just stencil paper ones with acrylic paint.

Butterfly Mobile

The butterflies in this mobile are made from mussel shells. You may not live near a beach where mussel shells can be collected, or have a garden where butterflies flutter about, but you can make this mobile that has a little bit of seaside and countryside in it.

If you have never tasted mussels before, this may be a chance to try them. Most fish-mongers sell mussels in their shells. When the mussels have been eaten, the shells are left, stuck together in the middle and already looking like butterflies. Scrub them well in warm soapy water.

YOU WILL NEED THESE MATERIALS AND TOOLS

7 mussel shells

Squeeze-on fabric paints, glitter, pearl or slick types

Gold paint and paintbrush

Pipe cleaners

Also 2 wooden boards, tin of paint for a weight, scissors, all-purpose clear adhesive, thin length of dowelling or garden cane, painted gold, and nylon thread

Fluttering in the breeze
Mobiles can be very relaxing to watch. Hang yours up above your bed and you will be able to drift off to sleep watching the butterflies gently turning in the air. Follow what Tania and Jade are doing and you will have a lovely mobile of fluttering butterflies.

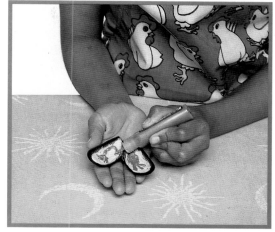

1 Don't try to open out dry mussel shells, or they will come apart. Instead, soak the shells in warm water overnight. Open them out gently and place them face down on a board. Cover with another board and weigh it down with something heavy, such as a tin of paint.

2 When the open shells have dried, decorate each one with a different pattern using the squeeze-on fabric paints. Practise on paper first to get the feel of squeezing the paint from the tubes. Look at pictures of butterflies – you will see how many different patterns you can use on your shell butterflies.

3 When the fabric paint is dry, turn the shells over and paint the dark side with gold paint.

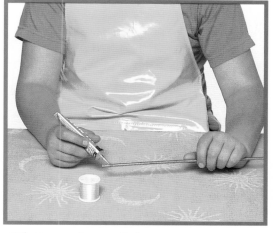

4 Cut up a pipe cleaner to make butterfly bodies about 4 cm (1½ in) long. Use glue to stick them in place.

5 Put a drop of glue 1 cm (½ in) in from each end of the stick, then knot the nylon thread over one of the dots. The glue stops the thread from slipping, making the knot easier to tie. Measure roughly double the length of the stick and cut and knot the nylon onto the glue dot at the other end. This is what the mobile hangs from.

6 Put seven dots of glue along the stick, 6 cm (2½ in) apart, and tie lengths of nylon over each dot. Tie the other ends of the nylon around the pipe-cleaner heads of each butterfly. Arrange them at different heights. It is very easy to tangle up the nylon threads so take care to keep each butterfly and its thread separate.

7 Seven very rare butterflies

Butterflies Everywhere

It would be most unusual to buy just seven mussels from the fishmonger, so you will probably have some left over. Decorate the shells with the paints and leave them to dry. Fix the bodies on as you did before and then glue them onto the corners of a picture frame or a mirror.

Feather Head-dress

The great Indian chiefs of North America wore head-dresses made from eagle feathers. They painted the feathers with patterns and each one had a special meaning, telling people how brave they were and how many battles they had won. Some chiefs wore head-dresses that reached all the way down their backs, from head to feet, called trailer war bonnets. When they held important gatherings or fought wars between the tribes, they would wear their feathers to show how brave and fierce they were. All the tribes understood the meaning of the feathers.

YOU WILL NEED THESE MATERIALS AND TOOLS

Piece of corrugated cardboard

Beads

String

Pasta quills

Pegs

Feathers, large and small

Elastic

Also scissors, ruler, white paper, PVA glue and felt-tipped pens

Magic feathers

Thomas and Edward are making this feather head-dress from seagull feathers, pasta quills, corrugated cardboard, beads and string. You can use any large feathers, so keep a look out when you go for a walk in the park or by the sea. If you live near a farm you can collect chicken or duck feathers.

Medicine men wore their feather head-dresses when they used their special powers, so perhaps you could wear yours and do a rain dance or, even better, a sunshine dance!

1 Cut the corrugated cardboard into a strip 4 cm x 25 cm (1½ x 10 in) and two discs 6 cm (2½ in) across. Cut white paper to match.

2 Glue the paper to the cardboard strip. Draw the beadwork pattern onto it with felt-tipped pens.

3 Glue the two paper discs to the cardboard discs. Decorate them with beadwork patterns.

4 Cut two lengths of string 18 cm (7 in) long. Thread beads onto each end of the string and make a knot below them.

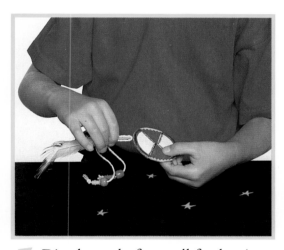

5 Dip the end of a small feather in the glue and use it to push the middle of the string up into a channel in the corrugated card disc. This is quite fiddly so ask a grown-up for help if you find it difficult.

6 Place a pasta quill on each large feather and push the ends down into the channels in the decorated cardboard strip. Arrange the biggest ones in the centre, using smaller ones towards each side.

7 Glue on the discs about 2.5 cm (1 in) from each end. Peg the pieces together until the glue has dried. Make a hole at each end of the strip and thread elastic through to fasten at the back.

Beautiful Beadwork

The North American Indians made wonderful clothes and jewellery from beads, feathers and strips of leather. They believed that every living thing on Earth was precious and many of the patterns they used for beadwork or weaving told stories of nature and the lives of their ancestors. Ask at your library for a book about them, and copy the beadwork patterns to make pictures using felt-tipped pens or crayons. Try making jewellery from strips of chamois leather (we use it for car washing) threaded with beads and tubes of pasta, like macaroni. And don't forget to do that sunshine dance!

Jewellery Box

Some packaging is just too good to throw away. If you have a baby sister or brother, there may be some empty "wet wipes" boxes which have hinged lids and a clasp to keep them shut. You can decorate them with pieces of felt and make a very special box to keep your jewellery in. Felt is easy to cut, and craft shops sell squares 30 x 30 cm (12 x 12 in) as well as small bags of scraps in different colours.

The zig-zag edge is made by using special scissors called pinking shears. Dressmakers use them, so ask a grown-up who you know does a lot of sewing if they have a pair you can borrow. Felt is such fun to cut out any-way, so if you don't have pinking shears just cut your own fancy edges with scissors.

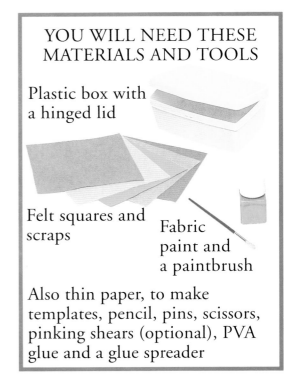

YOU WILL NEED THESE
MATERIALS AND TOOLS

Plastic box with
a hinged lid

Felt squares and
scraps

Fabric
paint and
a paintbrush

Also thin paper, to make templates, pencil, pins, scissors, pinking shears (optional), PVA glue and a glue spreader

This box belongs to ...
Everyone has favourite colours, so choose the ones you like best when you cover the box. Fabric paints come in all colours and are either pearly, puffy or shiny when they dry. You will need to practise writing to avoid making blobs. Kirsty is making a box for her friend Maria. You could write your name instead. Try it out a few times on differ-ent pieces of felt, and choose your best effort to stick on the box.

1 Make paper templates by drawing around the top, long and short sides of the box. Cut them out, but make the patterns a bit smaller if your box has raised edges like this one.

2 Use pins to hold the patterns and felt pieces together. Choose different colours of felt for the top and sides of the box.

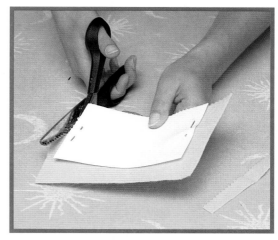

3 Cut out the felt pieces. Use pinking shears if you have them, or ordinary scissors if not. If you use pinking shears ask a grown-up to cut out the pieces of felt for you.

4 Stick the felt to the top and all the sides of the box.

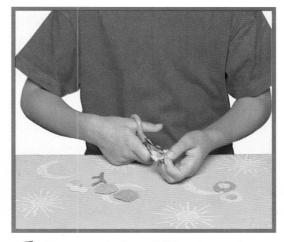

5 Cut out circles of felt, about 4 cm (1½ in) across for the flowers, and smaller ones for the flower centres. Stick the centres down and snip towards the centre to make petals. Cut out some flower stems too.

6 Glue the flowers to the top and sides of the box.

7 Using a paintbrush, write your name on a piece of felt with fabric paint. Try writing in small dots if lines seem too difficult.

Now that you have made it, you will probably need some new pieces of jewellery to go in your jewellery box!

Fun with Felt

If you enjoy snipping and gluing felt you could make a cover for your diary or a folder. Measure the shape and cut the background coloured felt to fit. Cut out shapes and patterns, letters and numbers, and glue them onto the background. Always make sure that the glue is spread evenly across the felt and right up to the edges.

Felt can be used on its own to make things too. A bookmark is useful. Just cut a long strip and snip 1 cm (½ in) into the ends to make a fringe.

Painted Flower-pot and Saucer

Everyone loves a gift that has been specially made for them. You may not be ready to make a flowerpot yet, but you could certainly decorate one as a special present.

Indoor plants can look dull in plain clay pots, especially the leafy ones without any flowers. This bright red and yellow pattern that Roxy is painting is very easy to do and is just the thing to brighten up a winter windowsill.

Preparing your pots

Clay pots need to be sealed before you can paint them, and PVA glue can be brushed on to give a good waterproof paint surface. When you paint stripes around a shape like a flowerpot, it is hard to keep the lines straight. A good trick is to put a rubber band around the pot wherever you need a guideline. It makes a slightly raised line to paint up to and can be slipped off when the paint is dry.

YOU WILL NEED THESE MATERIALS AND TOOLS

Houseplant

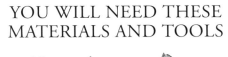

Clay flowerpot and saucer

Also PVA glue, to seal the surface of the pot, paintbrushes, acrylic paint – red and yellow, and a rubber band

1 Mix up three parts PVA glue with one part water and brush this all over the flowerpot and the saucer. Leave them to dry.

2 Paint the outside of the flowerpot and its inner rim and the outside of the saucer yellow. Mix acrylic paint with a little water, to make it thick and creamy. Leave it to dry and then paint on a second coat.

3 Stretch a rubber band around the flowerpot to mark the edge of the red section. Paint as shown in the picture. Leave the rubber band on until the paint is dry.

4 Make two red stripes with dots in-between them around the outer rim of the pot.

5 Paint the rim of the saucer red. Allow to dry. Then decorate the saucer with red spots on the yellow background and yellow spots on the red background.

6 Make yellow dots along the red stripes at the top of the pot. Paint yellow stripes down to the bottom edge, over the red. Paint big red dots in the middle and, when dry, put in smaller yellow dots. When all the paint has dried, seal the pot with the same PVA glue and water mixture that you started with in the first step.

A little bit of sunshine to put on the windowsill.

Go Potty Painting Pots!

Flowerpots come in all sizes and there are many different ways to paint them. Spots, stripes, wavy lines, diamonds, flowers – these are a few of the different shapes that you could use to make patterns. Stars look great too. Try making a stencil out of a piece of card. Cut out the shape with scissors and hold it firmly against the pot. Paint through the stencil, being careful to use only a tiny amount of paint on your brush.

Cork Rattlesnake

This cork and bead snake has a slithery feeling and will curl up or wriggle along, just like the real thing. Rattlesnakes get their name from the rattle at the end of their tail. They curl up and shake the rattle, holding their heads ready to strike when danger approaches. The rattling sound warns all creatures to beware as the rattlesnake is very dangerous.

Colourful crazy patterns

The corks used in this project have holes through the middle and are usually used for making home-made wines. You can buy them from large chemists and shops that specialize in winemaking equipment. Ordinary corks could be used, but you would have to ask an adult to drill holes through the middle of them for you.

Snake colours are brilliant and their patterns are exciting. Zig-zags, diamonds, stripes, swirls and spots are all very snaky. Look at what Reece and George have done and then have fun with your patterns and make a really unusual rattlesnake.

1 Paint all the corks green. Leave them to dry completely.

2 Paint the black pattern first. Then paint the red and yellow patterns in-between the black ones. Don't forget to decorate the ordinary cork that has been cut in half. This will be made into the mouth.

3 When the paint is dry thread the main body of the snake onto the elastic, with a bead between each cork. The corks are thicker at one end than the other. Make sure the tail cork tapers to the thin end.

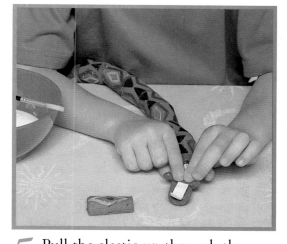

4 Thread five or six beads onto the end of the snake to make the rattle. Tie a knot at the end.

5 Pull the elastic up through the snake. Don't pull it too tight though, because the snake must be able to wriggle and roll up. Thread two beads onto the pipe cleaner to make the snake's eyes. Cut off the extra pipe cleaner leaving 1 cm (½ in) to twist and secure the beads in place. Flatten out the elastic so it runs along the flat side of the cork and sticks out at the end. Place the pipe cleaner across the elastic.

6 Paste with PVA glue and put the other half of the cork on top. Hold the two pieces together with a rubber band until the glue is dry.

Slithery Lizard

You could make a lizard out of corks. For the legs, ask a grown-up to make holes across two of the corks. Make the lizard up in the same way as the snake, then thread shorter pieces of elastic through the new holes. Thread three beads on each side and then a cork, with the wide end down. Add one more bead and tie a knot. Four corks added in this way will make four stubby lizard legs.

7 Cut the elastic into the shape of a forked tongue and paint red. The snake can be varnished with acrylic gloss or PVA glue diluted with water.

A slithery snake pet with no nasty nips.

Peanut and Macaroni Jewellery

YOU WILL NEED THESE MATERIALS AND TOOLS

Peanuts in shells

Macaroni

Beads

Darning needle and shirring elastic

Also paintbrushes, acrylic paints – red, blue, black and yellow, a cup, acrylic gloss varnish (optional) and PVA glue

Who needs gold, silver and diamonds when you have macaroni and peanuts in the kitchen cupboard? You can make the bright and chunky necklace and bracelet very easily and all your friends will want to make them too.

The peanuts look great painted in very bright primary colours, and are light and comfortable to wear. The macaroni is perfect for threading and makes a good space between the peanuts. Use acrylic paints which dry in five minutes, and give the nuts a good glossy varnish to make them shine.

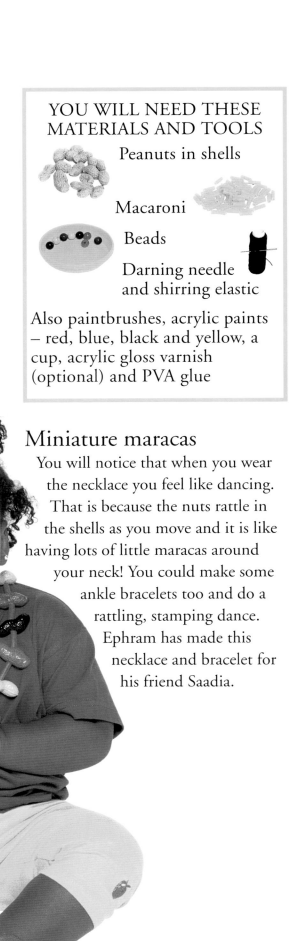

Miniature maracas

You will notice that when you wear the necklace you feel like dancing. That is because the nuts rattle in the shells as you move and it is like having lots of little maracas around your neck! You could make some ankle bracelets too and do a rattling, stamping dance. Ephram has made this necklace and bracelet for his friend Saadia.

1 Paint the peanuts different colours and leave to dry.

2 Mix some paint in a cup to colour the macaroni. Drop the macaroni in the cup and stir. Tip out and separate the pieces. Leave to dry.

3 When they are dry, varnish the nuts and macaroni with acrylic gloss varnish or PVA glue and water mixed three parts to one. Leave to dry.

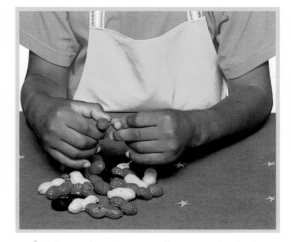

4 Use a darning needle to make holes through the middle of the peanuts. There is a hollow space between the two nuts, where the shell goes in at the "waist". Push the needle through both sides.

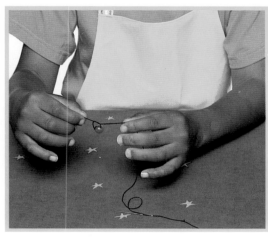

5 Measure around your neck and wrists and cut the shirring elastic just a bit longer. Thread the darning needle and tie a bead onto the end of the elastic.

6 Thread one piece of macaroni, then one nut and repeat the colours in the same order until you reach the end of the elastic.

7 Finish with a piece of macaroni and then tie on a bead. Tie the two beaded ends together.

What Else Could You Thread?

Popcorn can also be threaded to make jewellery. You will need home-made popcorn that has no salt or sugar coating. You can paint and varnish it with acrylics, just as you did with the peanuts.

Thread the darning needle and push it through the middle of the popcorn, where the burst outer shell is, as this is the strongest part. When you have threaded enough for a necklace, cut the elastic and tie a knot. You could try combining the macaroni, monkey nuts and popcorn. There are also lots of pips and seeds that thread easily, so have a good look in the store cupboard. Ask a grown-up if it is all right and then get threading.

Miniature Scarecrow

Farmers use scarecrows to trick the birds. A bird will not land in a field where the farmer is standing guard over his seeds and crops, so he makes a scarecrow in the shape of a man and sticks him in the ground. Sometimes this fools the birds and they stay away, but some birds are braver than others and fly down to have a closer look. These are the birds that you see sitting on the scarecrow's hat!

Happy in the house

The problem with this scarecrow is that he looks so happy and welcoming that the crows may just find him too friendly. Even if you are not bothered by lots of birds, this miniature scarecrow is such fun to make and he would look great on a window-ledge or bedroom bookshelf. Look how Rupert makes his scarecrow. The flowerpot filled with pebbles makes a sturdy base for him to stand in, and you will not even have to remember to water him either!

YOU WILL NEED THESE MATERIALS AND TOOLS

Turmeric to dye hair

Dishwashing mop

Sacking material, or hessian

Small flowerpot and pebbles

Also thin cardboard, scissors, felt-tipped pens, small yogurt pot, pencil, paintbrush, black acrylic paint, bamboo cane or doweling for the arms, 24 cm (10 in) long, rubber bands, PVA glue, coloured pipe cleaners and a feather.

1 Mix a heaped spoonful of turmeric with warm water and then swish the mop around in it. Squeeze out and hang up to dry overnight.

2 Cut a circle about 5.5 cm (2¼ in) across out of cardboard and draw the face with felt-tipped pens.

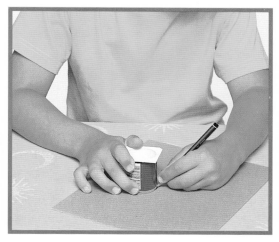

3 Draw a circle around the pot and then draw another one 3 cm (1¼ in) outside the first. Cut out the inside circle and then around the outer circle.

4 Slide the cardboard ring over the yogurt pot to make a hat with a brim, then paint the hat black with undiluted acrylic paint.

5 To make the clothes, cut a double square of sacking cloth 25 x 25 cm (15½ x 15½ in) with a fold at one edge. Trim the square into a rough T-shape and make a hole in the centre of the shoulder fold, for the stick.

6 Attach the arm cross-piece by looping and twisting a rubber band around both sticks, till it feels secure. Slide the arms up to the top of the stick and adjust them until they are the same length each side. Gather up the sacking around the stick and use a rubber band as a belt.

7 Stick the face onto the mophead. Make the hat decoration with twisted pipe cleaners and the feather.

8 Pour some of the pebbles into the pot. Push the stick through the hole in the bottom. Top up with pebbles.

A very jolly scarecrow.

Doll's House

The next time you visit a supermarket, choose a good strong cardboard box from the check-out to use to pack the shopping. When the groceries are all put away, you can use the box to make this doll's house.

You will need a grown-up to help with the first stages. Never use a craft knife on your own as the blades are dangerously sharp. The step photographs show how the box is cut, and you can help with a ruler and pencil, measuring and drawing the cutting guidelines, just as Kirsty is doing here.

Paint the house and roof with a light-coloured emulsion paint, the sort that is used to paint walls at home. This will make a good base coat for felt-tipped pens.

YOU WILL NEED THESE MATERIALS AND TOOLS

Sturdy cardboard box

Corrugated cardboard

Also light-coloured emulsion paint, paintbrushes, pencil, ruler, scissors, craft knife, adhesive tape, table knife, PVA glue, acrylic paints – red, yellow, and blue, paper, and felt-tipped pens

Moving in

This house is empty, and will need furnishing. Look for little boxes and tins to cover with fabric or felt as they will make good chairs. A carpet sample could be cut to fit inside, or you could colour paper to make a patterned rug. And to make the house your very own, you could write your house number on the door.

1 Paint the box. On both sides measure 10cm (4in) from the top. Find the middle point along the top edge. Join the dots and draw a triangle.

2 Ask a grown-up to cut out the shape of the house for you using big scissors or a craft knife.

3 The back of the house should be cut away so you can reach inside. Ask a grown-up to do this with the craft knife.

4 Use the side flaps to create the roof peak. Score the lines where they fold but don't cut right through. Stick the flaps down with adhesive tape.

5 To make the roof, measure the top of the box. Cut the corrugated cardboard so it is 2.5 cm (1 in) wider each side and 5 cm (2 in) longer at each end. Score down the central line with a table knife. Ask a grown-up to help you if you need to.

6 Bend the roof along the scored line. Paint the inside with PVA glue and place it on top of the house. When the glue is dry, paint the roof with yellow acrylic paint.

7 To make the windows, cut out squares of paper and paint the edges with blue acrylic paint. Cut out a front door and paint it red.

A pretty country house complete with cat, ready to be moved into and furnished.

Budding Architect

You could make lots of different buildings out of cardboard boxes. Perhaps you would like a garage to go with your house. You could even make a whole street of different buildings, including shops and a church.

Look for different sized boxes, such as shoe boxes, and other things. What could you use to make a post box, for example?

Pencil-pot Découpage

Pencils, pens and brushes roll off tables or slip down between the cushions of a sofa when you are concentrating hard on making pictures. You can organize yourself by making this pencil pot from a food tin with a ring-pull lid. Tin openers leave dangerously sharp edges, so be sure to choose the safer type with a ring-pull for this project.

The word découpage means "cutting out" in French. You cut out pictures and glue them to the object you are making. Furniture is some-times decorated in this way, and then given many coats of clear varnish. You can use clear acrylic varnish to give your pot a shine, or a mixture of PVA glue and water, mixed three parts to one.

YOU WILL NEED THESE MATERIALS AND TOOLS

Sheet of wrapping paper or other pictures

Empty tin, washed

Felt

Also blue paint, either acrylic or gloss, paintbrushes, scissors, PVA glue, soft cloth, acrylic gloss varnish (optional), small piece of corrugated cardboard and a pencil

Choosing your decorations

Jade has painted this tin blue and decorated it with cut-outs from a sheet of wrapping paper, but you could use the same method to make a pencil-pot to suit your own interests. Perhaps you have a comic-book character, pop star or sports person – someone whose picture you would like to see every day. Just cut out a combination of pictures that you like and glue them onto the painted tin. Take your time when cut-ting out, moving the paper to meet the scissors. It is a good idea to practise on a few spare sheets of paper before you cut out your most special pictures.

1 Paint the tin blue. Water-based paint is best, because you can wash your brushes under the tap. Acrylic will need two coats of undiluted paint.

2 Carefully cut out the motifs. The pattern looks best if you have two different sorts, such as butterflies and teddy bears.

3 Spread PVA glue over the back of each motif, making sure you reach all the outer edges. Otherwise the sides will curl up.

4 Stick down the motifs, using a soft cloth to flatten out any air bubbles. Arrange them around the tin with the same amount of space between them.

5 When the glue is dry, paint on acrylic varnish or a mixture of three parts PVA glue to one part water. The varnish can be gloss or matt.

6 Stand the tin on a piece of corrugated cardboard and draw around it. Cut out a circle, just inside the line, to fit into the base.

7 Draw a circle on the felt in the same way, but cut it out just outside the line. Stick the felt to the cardboard, then the cardboard to the pencil-pot with PVA glue.

Your very own, very organized decorated découpage pencil-pot!

What Else Deserves Découpage

You can cut out and stick all sorts of motifs onto all kinds of surfaces, not just tins. Wooden boxes, trays and bedroom furniture can all be brightened up with paper cut-outs, but always ask permission from a grown-up first. If you find a black and white picture or pattern that would make a good border, you can photocopy it as many times as you need. Cut out and colour your photocopies, and then glue them on.

35

Magnetic Fishing

This game is almost as much fun to make as it is to play. You could make it at your birthday party with each guest having a fish to decorate.

The fish shape is very simple, but your decoration can be as wild or realistic as you like. Roxy and Rupert like bright colours for their fish. Have a look at some fish in a shop or borrow a book about fish from your library – there are so many beautiful patterns and colours to choose from.

Playing your fish

Playing the fishing game can be as easy as dangling the magnet over them until you can lift a fish up with your rod. If you want to make it harder, you can write numbers of points on each fish, and write down each person's score. Put the side showing the numbers facing down, so that nobody knows which one scores the highest until it is caught. Some children play the game blindfolded, and are only given a short time, like 10 seconds, to catch one before the next person has a turn. There are already many different ways to play – perhaps you can invent some more.

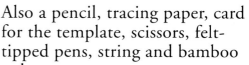

YOU WILL NEED THESE MATERIALS AND TOOLS

Fluorescent or coloured cardboard

Paper clips

Magnets

Also a pencil, tracing paper, card for the template, scissors, felt-tipped pens, string and bamboo poles

1 Find the fish template in the intro-
duction and follow the instructions
you will find there to trace and cut out
your pattern.

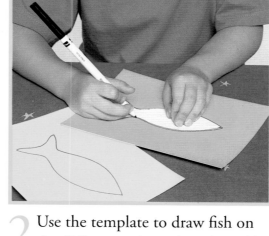

2 Use the template to draw fish on
the different coloured card. Hold
the template firmly so that it does not
move while you are drawing.

3 Cut out all your fish, taking care to
do this as neatly as possible.

4 Decorate the fish with different
coloured felt-tipped pens.

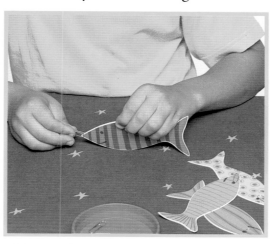

5 Attach the paper clips to the
mouths of the fish.

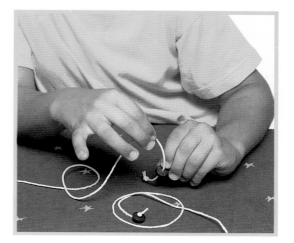

6 To make your fishing rods, tie a
magnet to each piece of string.

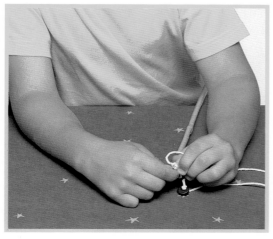

7 Then tie a piece of string onto the
end of each of the bamboo poles.

Roxy and Rupert have made a pond
where they can go fishing.

Other Magnetic Games

Magnetic fishing does not have to
involve fish. You could make sets of
different parts of the body – heads,
bodies, legs and arms. Some can be
girls and some boys and their clothes
can be as silly as you like. Put them all
in a box with paperclips attached and
take turns to fish for them. It will be
like a game of picture consequences
when you have to fit your person
together. Alternatively you could fish
for letters to make words, or pictures of
food to make up dinners.

Birdwatchers

If you have ever seen birdwatchers, you'll have noticed that they are very quiet and slow-moving. Any sharp movements or noises would frighten the birds and they would fly away.

These binoculars are green so they are camouflaged as you creep around the park or garden birdwatching. Stay very still and the birds will come quite close. If you have a bird-bath or table in your garden, the birds that use it will be quite tame, so they might not mind even if they do see you watching.

Sunny all the time

These binoculars have a very special feature. They brighten up dull days, making the world outside look sunny, even when it's grey. George has found some sweets with yellow cellophane wrappers – just the thing to cover the ends of his binoculars.

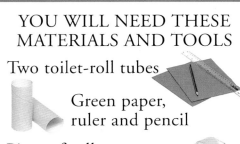

YOU WILL NEED THESE
MATERIALS AND TOOLS

Two toilet-roll tubes

Green paper,
ruler and pencil

Piece of yellow
cellophane

Adhesive tape

Black plastic tape

Black cord

Also scissors, a wine cork, PVA glue, paintbrush, black acrylic paint and a rubber band

1 Cut out two squares of cellophane and tape them over one end of each cardboard tube. Ask a grown-up to help if you find this difficult.

2 Cut out two rectangles of green paper measuring 12 x 19 cm (4½ x 7½ in). Then cut a strip of paper to fit around the cork.

3 Ask a grown-up to trim the cork lengthways , so that one half has two flat sides. Paint the ends with black acrylic paint.

4 Take the strip of green paper and glue it around the cork. Paint on lines for the focusing winder.

5 Brush the pieces of green paper with glue. Line up with the tube ends without cellophane, then roll the tubes onto the paper.

6 Stick black plastic tape around the ends with the cellophane, then trim the paper and tape close to the cellophane ends.

7 Spread a stripe of glue along the side of one tube, and both flat sides of the cork. Assemble the binoculars, and hold them together with a rubber band until the glue is dry.

8 Push a hole through the sides of each tube, and thread the black cord through. Tie a knot on the inside.

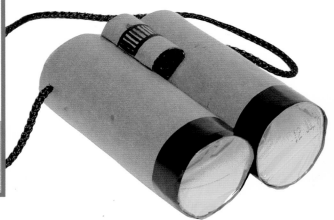

Now you are ready to go birdwatching – and the weather looks just fine!

Monster Sock Puppet

Everyone has an odd sock somewhere around the house, waiting to be brought to life as a monster sock puppet. Try to find one that is brightly coloured and use a contrasting colour felt for the mouth and fins. Kirsty has practised her monster noises, because she is going to need them!

Pins and needles

If you have never used a sewing needle before, be sure to ask a grown-up to help you. Sewing is quite easy, once you know how, and you will not need to use a very sharp needle to sew through felt and sock material. A darning needle will do the job.

If you use pins to hold the mouth lining in place as you sew it, be very careful, because they are sharp. Always position them so their points are facing in the same direction around the monster's mouth. When you start to sew, work towards the heads, not the points, of the pins. Each time you reach a pin, remove it and put it back in a pin cushion or tin, so that nobody gets a sharp surprise!

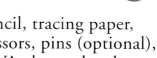

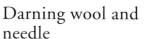

1 Trace the template for the mouth which you will find in the intro-duction. Cut it out to make a pattern. Put this on a folded piece of felt, so that the fold is along the straight edge of the pattern. Cut out the mouth and the other shapes. Just nip the felt to make zig-zags, spiky fins, and a tongue.

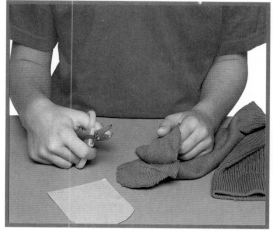

2 Turn the sock inside-out and cut along the toe seam and past it on both sides by about 5 cm (2 in). Measure the opening against the pattern for the mouth, to get the size right.

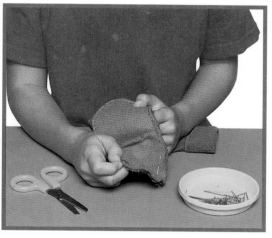

3 Pin the mouth lining into the toe end, flapping the top back, so that you can sew the lining in one flat piece. Sew along the seam using running stitches. Make a small cut along the fold of the mouth and poke the tongue through it, so that it sticks out on the other side. Sew the tongue in place.

4 Turn the sock right side out and sew on buttons for eyes. Use wool to do this, pushing the needle up from inside the sock, through the holes and back down again. Tie the ends of wool inside the sock.

5 Stick on the nostrils, spreading PVA glue across the back of the felt, right up to the edges. Stick on triangles and zig-zags in the same way.

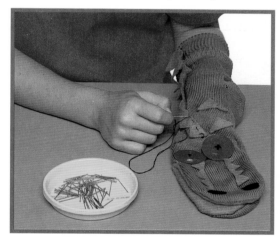

6 Sew the long back fin along the centre of the monster's back, using black thread or wool. Be careful not to prick your hand with the needle.

Now is the time to use those monster noises that you have been practising!

Shark Alert!

There are all kinds of creatures to be made from odd socks. If you have a grey sock you could try making a shark. You will need grey felt for the fins and red for the mouth lining. Nice white teeth are a very important feature, so cut them from felt and fit them into the mouth at the same time as the lining. Think carefully as they will need to stick up from the shark's gums. So cut triangles and sew the flat ends into the mouth seam, leaving the pointy teeth to stick up in the mouth. To make the big back fin, cut two triangles and put a bit of cotton wool stuffing in-between them. Sew around the edges and then sew the base of the fin into the middle of the back.